What's awake?

Bats

Patricia Whitehouse

www.raintreepublishers.co.uk
Visit our website to find out more information about **Raintree** books.

To order:
☎ Phone 44 (0) 1865 888112
🖹 Send a fax to 44 (0) 1865 314091
💻 Visit the Raintree Bookshop at raintreepublishers.co.uk to browse our catalogue and order online.

First published in Great Britain by Raintree, Halley Court, Jordan Hill, Oxford OX2 8EJ, part of Harcourt Education.
Raintree is a registered trademark of Harcourt Education Ltd.

Editorial: Nick Hunter and Diyan Leake
Design: Sue Emerson (HL-US) and Joanna Sapwell (www.tipani.co.uk)
Picture Research: Susana Darwin (HL-US) and Maria Joannou
Production: Lorraine Hicks

Originated by Dot Gradations
Printed and bound in China by South China Printing Company

ISBN 1 844 21354 4
07 06 05 04 03
10 9 8 7 6 5 4 3 2 1

British Library Cataloguing in Publication Data
Whitehouse, Patricia
Bats
599.4
A full catalogue record for this book is available from the British Library.

Acknowledgements
The publishers would like to thank the following for permission to reproduce photographs: Animals Animals p. 7 (E. R. Degginger); Corbis p. 23 (mammal); David Liebman p. 9 (Roger Rageot); Heinemann Library p. 23 (roof, Sue Emerson); Photo Researchers, Inc. pp. 5 (B. G. Thompson), 8, 13 (Merlin D. Tuttle/Bat Conservation International), 14 (Merlin D. Tuttle/Bat Conservation International), 15 (Merlin D. Tuttle/Bat Conservation International), 16 (Merlin D. Tuttle/Bat Conservation International), 17 (Merlin D. Tuttle/Bat Conservation International), 18 (Stephen Dalton), 19 (B. G. Thompson), 21 (Merlin D. Tuttle/Bat Conservation International), 22 (B. G. Thompson), 23 (fur, Merlin D. Dalton; nocturnal, E. R. Degginger), back cover (moth, Merlin D. Tuttle/Bat Conservation International; wing, B. G. Thompson); Visuals Unlimited pp. 4 (Steve Strickland), 6 (Joe McDonald), 10 (Richard Thom), 11 (Joe McDonald), 12 (Joe McDonald), 20 (Richard C. Johnson), 23 (colony, Richard Thom).

Cover photograph of bats, reproduced with permission of Photo Researchers, Inc.

Every effort has been made to contact copyright holders of any material reproduced in this book. Any omissions will be rectified in subsequent printings if notice is given to the publishers.

CAUTION: Remind children that it is not a good idea to handle wild animals. Children should wash their hands with soap and water after they touch any animal.

Some words are shown in bold, **like this.** You can find them in the glossary on page 23.

Contents

What's awake?

Some animals are awake when you go to sleep.

Animals that stay awake at night are **nocturnal**.

Bats are awake at night.

What are bats?

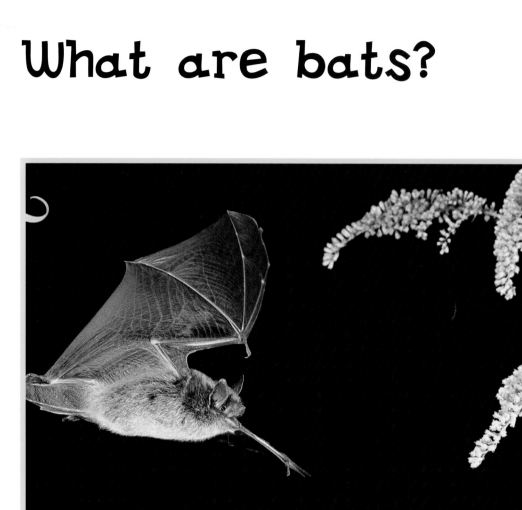

Bats are **mammals** that can fly.

baby bat

Mammals have **fur**.

Mammal babies drink milk from their mother's body.

What do bats look like?

wing

Bats look like mice with big wings.

Their wings are covered with skin.

Some bats are as small as
your hand.

Other bats have wings as wide
as a man's arms.

Where do bats live?

Bats' homes are called **roosts**.

They live in groups called **colonies**.

In the wild, bats live in caves or trees.

In cities, bats live under **roofs** or bridges.

What do bats do at night?

Bats wake up just before dark.

They start to move around
and fly a bit.

They fly away to look for food.

Bats can eat all night.

What do bats eat?

Most bats eat moths.

They eat other bugs, too.

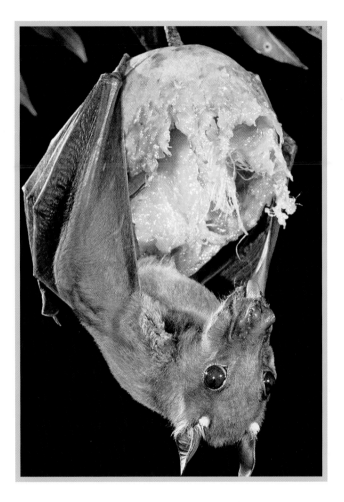

Many bats eat fruit.

This bat is eating a melon.

What do bats sound like?

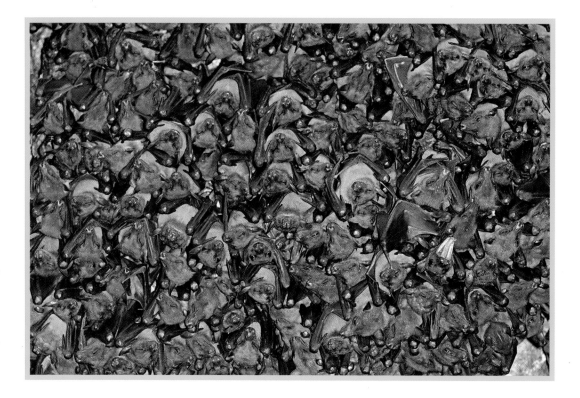

Bats make two kinds of noise.

One noise is a squeaking sound.

The other noise helps bats to find food.

Scientists need to use machines to hear this noise.

How are bats special?

Bats use a special noise to find bugs.

The sound bounces off the bugs, so the bat can tell where they are.

Bats hang upside down to sleep.

Where do bats go during the day?

In the morning, bats fly back to their **roosts**.

Bats take care of their babies.

Then they go to sleep.

Bat map

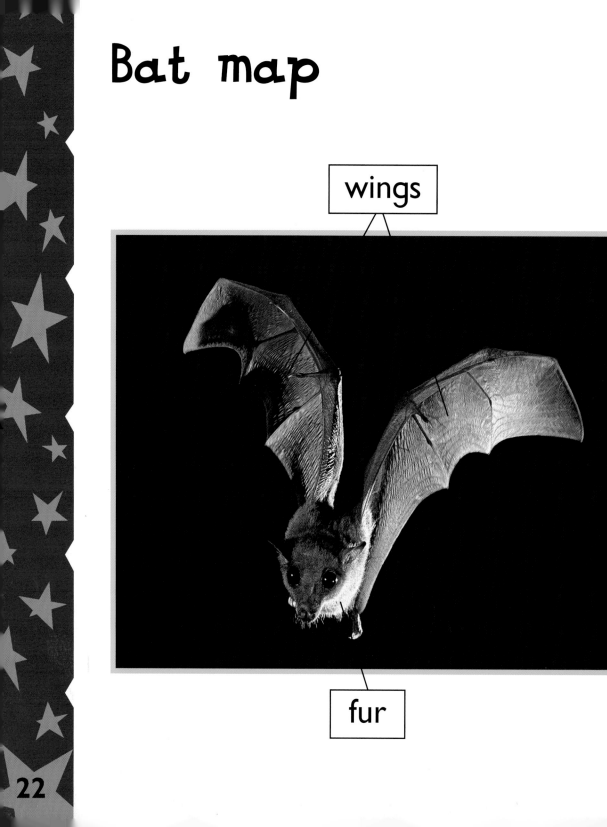

wings

fur

Glossary

colony
group of bats

fur
soft, short hair

mammal
animal that is covered in fur and feeds its
babies with milk from its own body

nocturnal
awake at night

roof
part that covers the top of a house

roost
place where a bat colony lives

scientist
person who works to find out things
about the world

Index

Titles in the What's Awake? series include:

Hardback   1 844 21353 6

Hardback   1 844 21354 4

Hardback   1 844 21352 8

Hardback   1 844 21355 2

Find out about the other titles in this series on our website www.raintreepublishers.co.uk